ETEL ADNAN

THE ARAB APOCALYPSE

THE ARAB APOCALYPSE was first published in French in 1980 by the Editions Papyrus, Paris, France, under the title *L'Apocalypse Arabe*. The present English version is the author's own translation from the original French.

Some of these poems have appeared in *Red Bass* and *Compages*.

The Library of Congress has catalogued the original edition as follows:

Adnan, Etel.
    The Arab apocalypse.

    Translation of: L'Apocalypse arabe.
    I. Title
PQ3939.A3A813   1989   841   88-32305
ISBN 0-942996-09-7 (original)
ISBN 978-0-942996-60-9 (3rd edition)

Copyright © by Etel Adnan 1989
Foreword © 2006 by Jalal Toufic
All rights reserved

Simone Fattal, Publisher
The Post-Apollo Press
35 Marie Street
Sausalito, California 94965

Cover drawing and book design by Etel Adnan
Composed by Michael Sykes at Archetype West, Point Reyes Station, California

10 9 8 7 6 5 4

Printed in the United States of America on acid-free paper.

ETEL ADNAN

THE ARAB APOCALYPSE

With a Foreword by Jalal Toufic

The Post-Apollo Press

BY THE SAME AUTHOR

Moonshots, Beirut 1966

Five Senses for One Death, The Smith, New York 1971

"Jebu" suivi de "L'Express Beyrouth—> Enfer," P.J. Oswald, Ed., Paris 1973

Pablo Neruda Is a Banana Tree, De Almeida, Lisbon 1982

From A to Z, The Post-Apollo Press, 1982

Sitt Marie-Rose, The Post-Apollo Press, 1982

The Indian Never Had a Horse & Other Poems, The Post-Apollo Press, 1985

Journey to Mount Tamalpais, The Post-Apollo Press, 1986

The Spring Flowers Own & The Manifestations of the Voyage, The Post-Apollo Press, 1990

Paris, When It's Naked, The Post-Apollo Press, 1993

Of Cities & Women (Letters to Fawwaz), The Post-Apollo Press, 1993

There: In the Light and the Darkness of the Self and of the Other, The Post-Apollo Press, 1997

In / somnia, The Post-Apollo Press, 2002

In the Heart of the Heart of Another Country, City Lights Books, 2005

ETEL ADNAN

THE ARAB APOCALYPSE

Resurrecting the Arab Apocalypse STOP [THE WORLD][1]

From time to time, there occurs what suspends time, revelation—at least for certain people, martyrs. But then the apocalypse, revelation, is withdrawn, occulted by the "apocalypse," the surpassing disaster, so that symptomatically *apocalypse*'s primary sense (from Greek *apokalypsis*, from *apokalyptein* to uncover, from *apo-* + *kalyptein* to cover) is occulted by its secondary meaning, and *martyr*'s primary sense, *witness*, is occulted by its secondary, vulgar meaning: "a person who suffers greatly or is killed because of their political or religious beliefs." One of the symptoms of such a surpassing disaster is that one of the Twentieth Century's major Arabic books of poetry, Etel Adnan's *L'Apocalypse Arabe*, published in 1980, has been out of print for around two decades. *L'Apocalypse Arabe*, an Arab book of poetry?! Notwithstanding that it was written originally in French (1980) then rewritten in English (1989) by an author who lives for the most part in the USA and France, it is an Arab book of poetry in part because it was withdrawn, occulted by the surpassing disasters that have affected the Arab world. A small number of Arab writers, video makers, filmmakers and artists, some of whom live abroad, have been working to resurrect, make available again what has been withdrawn by the Arab "apocalypse," including Adnan's *L'Apocalypse Arabe*. Have they succeeded? Adnan's book is here being reprinted in English—if the current date of reprint of this book that's untimely except in its relation to the surpassing disaster is timely and therefore symptomatic, this reissue would indicate the

---

[1] On *stopping the world*, see Carlos Castaneda's *Journey to Ixtlan: The Lessons of Don Juan*.

book's resurrection. The reader is soon alarmed by the repeated telegraphic STOP of this book that orbits the following doomed objects: the Sun and Tall al-Zaʿtar and Quarantina, two refugee camps that were besieged and criminally destroyed during the Lebanese civil war ("the Quarantina is torching its inmates STOP", "7 thousand Arabs under siege thirsty blinded STOP… 7 thousand Arabs in the belly of vultures STOP"). While the Arab "apocalypse" as surpassing disaster leads to a withdrawal of Arabic tradition, the apocalypse as revelation leads to Arabic tradition's vertiginous extension, so that it comes to include many a bodhisattva as well as many a schizophrenic/psychotic who is not an Arab by descent and/or birthplace but who exclaims in his or her dying before dying: "Every name in history is I" (Nietzsche). Due to this apocalyptic extension of tradition, one has—away from the cumulative shade of the many "100% Lebanese" banners that were raised during the massive demonstration that took place in Beirut on 14 March 2005 in indignant commemoration of the assassination of former prime minister Rafîq al-Harîrî a month earlier—an anamnesis, recollecting, as an anarchist, that "the sun is a Syrian king riding a horse from Homs to Palmyra open skies preceding" (cf. Antonin Artaud's *Heliogabalus; or, The Crowned Anarchist*, 1933), and, as an ancient Egyptian, "a yellow sun crammed in a boat," etc. A poet whose country and its refugee camps were being shattered by explosions during its protracted civil war managed nonetheless, perhaps because she poetically felt, like Judge Schreber with his solar anus and his singular cosmology, "a sun in the rectal extremity" and "a sun in the arms in the anus," to heed this news, "The radio says History allocated 10 billion years to the sun / ▰ the SUN has already lived half its age," and, while Frank Tipler and other Western physicists were trying to devise long-term emergency measures to deal with the future explosion of the scientific age's Sun, a yellow dwarf of spectral type G2, screamed: "An Apocalyptic sun explodes." Have Arabs, who, with very rare exceptions, continue to indulge in their petty concerns, taken notice? Was it enough to have *The Arab Apocalypse* translated into Arabic in 1991 for it to be read in the Arab world once it is resurrected? Even before having it translated to Arabic by someone else, it seems that the author, also an artist, had already partly translated it into graphic signs for the so many Arabs (38.7 per cent in 1999, or about 57.7 million adult Arabs [UN's *Arab Human Development Report* 2002]) who are illiterate, for whom Arabic is as illegible as English and French—may they be jolted by its graphic signs… into, at last but not least, learning to read—and then actually read (doesn't the great Seventh Century Arabic apocalyptic book, which has reached us through the prophet Muhammad, enjoin us to do so?).

— *Jalal Toufic*

I

A yellow sun   A green sun   a yellow sun   A red sun   a blue sun
a ✷ sun   A sun ✶ a ◉ blue a ⋯ red a ◉ blue
a blue yellow sun a yellow red sun a blue green sun a
a yellow boat a yellow sun a ◉ red a ◉ red blue and yellow
a yellow morning on a green sun a flower flower on a blue blue but
a yellow sun A green sun a yellow sun A red sun a blue sun
a ✻ yellow A sun ✻ a small craft ⊿ a boat ≋ a ⁂ red   blue

a quiet blue sun on a card table a red which is blue and a wheel
A solar sun a lunar sun a starry sun a nebular sun
A yellow sun   A green sun a yellow sun Qorraich runner ran running
A blue sun before a red sun   a green sun before a lunar sun
A floral sun ✾ a small craft as round as a round sun ●   A solar moon

Another sun jealous of Yellow enamoured of Red terrified by Blue horizontal
A sun romantic as Yellow jealous as Blue amorous as a cloud   ≣
A frail sun a timid sun ◉ vain sorrowful and bellicose sun
A Pharaonic ⌒ boat an Egyptian sun a solar universe and a universal sun

A solar arrow crosses the sky An eye dreads the sun the sun is an eye
A tubular sun haunted by the tubes of the sea ∽ a sun pernicious and vain
A ⊕ Hopi a Red Indian sun an Arab Black Sun a sun yellow and blue

a solar Hopi a solar Indian reddening a solar Arab darkening
a solar cord a musical Greek a rosace ⚘ solar a sun in an old sky
a sun in the room a room ✳ in a ◡ sun rolling on the sky
a blue sky for a ▢ yellow sun a yellow sky for ⟿ a blue sun
a blue tattoo in the sky a sun tattoed with sins   solar sins
a Bedu sunstruck a ⚚ sun-sick and the sea drowing the sea
a sun alarmed alarming the color yellow the yellow alarming sun moon and sea
a militant tattoo a militant sun in a warm ⁑ universe ⚘ a straight sun
a solar craft under the Nile the Nile crossing a sun the sun laughing
a solar imbecile a lunar cloud a polar woman a sun ultra brave
a ✦ sun solar nocturnal fluvial bestial choleric and yellow as yellow
an egg yolk sun confined to an asylum tearing its skin into lightning
a solar craft under the Nile the Nile crossing a sun the sun ⬬ laughing
a sunlike and solar tattoo is an Arab eye in the middle of the Milky Way
A ✦ maddeningly yellow another peacefully green a blue terror   O moon!   ⟿
A yellow and quiet sun on a quiet and soft horizon next to flowers. Everyday
A sun victory of the yellow on the green of the green ⁑ over the yellow in
                              the meadow of tears.

II

A yellow sun a sun ⟶ toward the sea a sun reckless and in love with the sea
a   meritorious   lightning-rod going to the heart of a lemon
a purple sun over a planetary volcano   O   Mexico!   bed undone over a   flower

O moon non solar O woman non Egyptian O royal and solar council of kings!
       great Inca O ant-like sun and blue ant in front of a red cat!
       giant Hopi hopping on a dynosaur blue green sun bitter misfortune
war vessel yellow sun peace vessel yellow sun motion
       boredom's trajectory on the mobile wall   O white hospital!!!
       moon as green as frozen leaf under the avalanche of a solar   star
a black sun a   still black black ink black light blue silk   tree
a black tree a palm tree black and inky like a tower   the silk of trees
a yellow sun in an egg and the sea in tears a child as yellow as the sun
a tattoo on the belly a sun in the rectal extremity an eye   the cut ear of the moon

a moon atrocious a yellow crime flower on   a bird's wing
a crime thrice solar toes caressed by the flux   red Pacific Ocean
the sun is a Syrian king riding a horse from Homs to Palmyra open skies preceding

a sun sunning the bed the bed of a nocturnal river   season!!!
a Hopi filled with bitter whiskey a solar bar in the midst of America   anthracite
a sun as androgynous as yellow mixed to blue   red and blue bird
a yellow sun a purple sun   in the purple heat of the wind
        an Indian sun a Hindu sun a Zoroastrian sun a sun for catacombs
my pain mounting the sun like a racing horse. The field is infinite
    a yellow sun claimed like a melon from Amazonia   O dead Indians!
a red sun a black sun a yellow sun a purple sun and nothing else
O thwarted Arabian moon   orgiastic under the rain the wind hou ! hou! the desert
morning sun solar morning banal morning   apotheosis. An angel went by . . .
sun risen as early as an arm bewitched universe   teapot full of atoms
a yellow sun in my memory cancer in the heart of the rose the prisoner's cry
O sun which tortures the Arab's eye in the Enemy's prison! Sun yellow silence.

III

The night of the non-event. War in the vacant sky. The Phantom's absence.
Funerals. Coffin not covered with roses. Unarmed population. Long.
The yellow sun's procession from the mosque to the vacant Place. Mute taxis.
Plainclothed army. Silent hearse. Silenced music. Palestinians with no Palestine.

The night of the Great Inca did not happen. Engineless planes. Extinguished sun.
Fishermen with no fleet fish with no sea fleet with no fish sea without fishermen
Guns with faded flowers Che Guevara reduced to ashes. No shade.
The wind neither rose nor subsided. The Jews are absent. Flat tires.
The little lights are not lit. No child has died. No rain
I did not say that spring was breathing. The dead did not return.

The mosque has launched its unheeded prayer. Lost in the waves.
The street lost its stones. Brilliant asphalt. Useless roads. Dead Army.
Snuffed is the street. To shut off the gas. Refugees with no refuge no candle.
The procession hasn't been scared. Time went by.   Silent Phantom.

Stagnant tide. Weightless blackness. Motionless cold around a non-existent fire.
Car with no driver Achrafieh-Hamra words under lock. Fear with no substance.
Windowless walled City.　　　　A dead man forced to go home on foot. A bullet in the
　　　　　　　　　　　　　　　　　　　　　　　　　　　　　　　　　　　belly.

Prayer in the mosque. Black procession tinier than ants. Allahu Akbar.
　　　　　Cybernetics of Doom broken machine. A breeze but no garden.
The much awaited enemy has not come. He ate his yellow sun and vomited.
Time: lemon crushed by a wheel grating under funerals
Between Beirut and Sidon there is the sea. This night is not of war.
Nothing is crushed by the Silence. Guns are rusting in travel bags. Revolution.

IV

A yellow sun in the gully red wine blood zebra stripes in the solar sky!!!
a green sun streaked with Indians O massacre in splendor!!
overheated sun furnace voyage in petrolic gardens O slumber!
a solar level a solar country a solar tribe sshu a valley's flank

a yellow world a blue sun a yellow sun eternal vertigo in my hand
a nilotic sluice stopping the sun the moon terrified O crushed legend???!

a sun ??? yellow ??? a ??? sun ??? green ??? a ? boat ? blue and pink
solar star on the forehead and the moon for an eye pharaoh's tomb
O fear O pain   spinal cord plundered by the conquest
Solar palm tree immense cancer on a milky way the Constellations of Sorrow

a yellow sun over Mexico trembles. Mexico trembles. sleeps the sun
a green sun and a solar green the slowness of the solar boats along your arm
a world I rolled as grass ate the slug my flowers are cut
a Nubian nubile spring rape of almond trees in no-flowers. Diaphanous flowers.
an Arab tortured mutilated vomits the sun hangs from his feet. Meticulously.

a yellow sun a blue sun a purple sun a green sun
a Jerusalem the Lord's house of shame   a calcinated Jerusalem Jerusalem of glass!

a sun did you say yellow did you say a sun did you say yellow you didn't say?

astral television ⊙ thundering ball kissing a worm   purple sun and . . .

A green sun on the Meadow of Tears # sun in my pocket   wretched pocket sun

a yellow sun a dust noise point point point a point and a blue circle
O fear O pain   sun settled in my head and eyes of toys
a sun   glacial nocturnal gardenal pentothal dialectical and Yemenite
Yemen yellow like pollen from the Yemen and snow from the Sierra. The day's death
     a yellow sun O   colorless vertigo ⁞⁞⁞⁞ the sun eating almond trees

a solar palm   museums sarcophagi and rot   the sea is widowed. Yes.
a tearful sun doped with roses swims in nebulae now
    green and purple destroy bone marrow in an inkpot ⊂⊃ crushed horizon
a universe waiting solar sun knocking at the door eating its own words
a deicide sun. There is a rallye in yellow chaos
a sun lying on the highway a sheriff checking its heart. Have a good laugh.
??? when the bordello opened its door ↶ ↶ ↶ they found the sun fucking
a yellow sun yawns over Beirut and Paris is dying and New York is fainting. O unsewn Time!

V

A yellow sun 🌀   my father an assassin I have a sun on each finger   head hair
                                              thick head of hair
a red sun a noise solar and red 🎵 in the sky a fragment from a tree
   the Hopi Indian holding his sexual organ divine pee for funeral oration
a sun goes through your eye two black wings   O yellow tumefied sun!
boat on the lagoon sun on the canal sailboat on the bay galleon on the channel
blue waters bestride the amazon moon O Amazonia without /// Indians!
the Amazon moon is catching fire green sun blue sun my mother's potbellied fish
    decapitated sun series of stars yellow sun rocket   Mad Mad Mad Mad
a solar fool an insane sun solar insanity an insane sun solar insanity insane sun

My yellow insanity green mud in my veins calcified sun a radar went insane
yellow green red purple   cosmic radar   a solar naked and insane man
a sun blue in a black sky a sun young in a black root   YES   ززز
a woman solar a woman lunar a female sun   snow put into digits

a sun yellow and desperate a market place for the sun
a sun sold in Mexico peeled in Borneo maimed in Beirut   Vom
a sun skinned a moon sodomized a brain unhinged a dog electrocuted!!?

a sun yellow green sleepwalker a sleepwalker stricken with sleep

an open space a number a woman crucified with flowers. One and one to nothing.
The moon left Amazonia an Inca licking her feet the sun watching
a corpse carried straight up through jungles O school for snakes charming the charmer!

A yellow sun   rising and murdered ↡↡ tooth-ache   a tree white and in bloom

The sun is my dispersed childhood's tree   sunset with no morning no night. BLACK.

A blue sun streaked with purple lonely lonely   more than widowed. Lone.

O moaning HOU HOU HOU like wind in the belly HOU HOU HOU HOU HOU MORE THAN
                                                                                                                          WIDOWED

sun-telephone. Sun thick tomb's silence telephone silence. SPIDER.

a drugged morphine-craving sun   the ascension of the mountain   the distance from the sea

a solar drug an open mushroom a mushrooming sun a red drug
a black sun mating a red sun   black radar in your black eye. SPIDER

a sun weary of rolling a sun tossed away a sick sun shining through its agony.

16

VI

Sun of Wichitah!   burns the single corn stalk in Wichitah! The mayor's phallus
One sun in Wichitah Three bulls in Cheyenne STOP my thoughts emerge
O disaster STOP O sun STOP O bliss STOP STOP a broken engine
an eye rounded and yellowed by the prison STOP San Quentin streams under the sun
a solar boat a palm tree in the refrigerator and the Cordillera under my arm

Voyage to the hollow of a valley in the center   of my memory   sulfuric burns

I tell the sun's story it answers I decode it sends new messages   I decode

from the center of the sun a tree sends a message BZZ BZZ BZZ BZZZZ a cancer grows

On its neck the tree carries cancer but a solar cancer solar baby
A yellow sun crammed in a boat   a vessel with melon-soft belly a kiss

Lagoon La Paz the Sea of Cortez blue ink on a rock. Sharp-edged is the ocean
The sea is green so is the mother with tooth-ache and amputation. Artaud-Torture

A sun from Diarbekyr a gully under the ramparts and sonorous boats
a sun from Mardin and the spring exploded O the purple velvet of the hills!
a Turkish sun an Arab sun a Kurdish sun a Hindu-owlish sun

a solar morning on the Euphrates   Wichitah is crying in the King's vagina
a pink sun a day as single as a cherry-flower mounting an elephant
O disaster ●)   a solar boat tattoo on my belly and rice fields
There are rice fields in my hair a sun in my nostrils STOP STOP
Folly round and round ●)   in the navel of the drawer   One two three four
green sun purple sun a sun in Messi Messaoud black sun
a sun full of gas and petrol   of fuel oil alcohol and tears
egg yolk sun locked into an asylum STOP a night in Gaziantep
a variegated woman sitting on tombs under the sun's gaze
My life a highway driven by armies General Sun is devastating
a victorious sun vertigo at the bed's foot and staircases tumbling down   ←   > ——†←
sun ambulance siren collapsing stars and a rainful of milky ways O silence!
a sun cutting Syria in two   gassing trees   black bird from Suvar

a stream is singing under the youthful grass a horse is coming home and the sun is passing by . . .

18

VII

A warring sun in Beirut thunderous April cool breeze on the ships
yellow sun on a pole an eye in the gun's hole a dead from Palestine
a purple sun in my friend's pocket meanderings in PARIS
a bird on a dead Palestinian's toe a fly at the butchery
Beirut-sulphuric-acid STOP the Quarantina is torching its inmates STOP Beirut
a sun on the finger a sun in the gut a sun climbing an elephant
cannibal anthropophagus sun wart on the cargoes ! ! ! ! !
a yellow sun on the face cancer on the Palestinian cruelty of the palm tree
I led a ship under the sea to the living and the dead   yes   yes   yes
a black sun 45 black corpses for a single coffin black eye listening
I saw a hawk eat a child's brain in the dumps of Dekouaneh

A dead sun was a toy in Sabra   I cut the sky in two

a sun rotten and eaten by worms floats over Beirut   silence is sold by the pound

Bedouins covered by sarcophagi know that a tattooed moon floods you with dynamite!

the sun blown-up a child blown-up a fish blown-up the street blown-up
eat and vomit the sun eat and vomit the war hear an angel explode

a bestial sun crawls on my backbone and gnaws at my neck. Its hair . . .
Its hair is falling Outside fascism dressed in green masturbates its guns

O backfired adventure! I saw Beirut-the-fool write with blood Death to the moon!

A rocket shatters the house. Bullets fly. They rip up a store. They stampede a cat

I took the sun by the tail and threw it in the river. Explosion. BOOM . . .

Beirut syphilis carrying whore   the sun is contaminated by the city

a blue sun receding a Kurd killing an Armenian an Armenian killing a Palestinian . . . ● ● ● ●
the solar wheel of Syrian races O insane nomads drinkers of dust
a hydrophilic sun a hilarious yellow sun red and vain red sun
Beirut-the-Mean a Party drunk with petroleum militia in whirlpools

a sun in a belly full of vegetables a system of fat tuberosis a sun which is SOFT

the eucalyptus are in bloom. the Arabs are under the ground. the Americans on the moon.

the sun has eaten its children   I myself was a morning blessed with bliss.

VIII

The sun a pool of blood. A corpse lying in the sun   HOU ! HOU !
A yellow sun   the ocean is a balloon deflating its vomit
an adolescent died on the surface of the horizon. How blue is the sea !
an anemic sun loses a tooth a day   STOP   the war
the war laid its flowers under tombs. Red for the unspilled blood
the war sprouted like a cactus between my toes   It's five o'clock

Treason floats down the smooth surface of the Euphrates like a woman
the sun's fingers are sawed and the moon is patient. I'm leaving.
a sun tattooed with lies spilling over your legs
Who prevents us from kissing? A dead snake in the sun.
a solar sun a solar moon a solar river and that's all
a funeral sun carried over a headless body a Kurd watching
despicable Arabian sun triumphant Arabian sun   vanquished sun
a sun as lonesome as a fish with no baggage   a train
the Arabian sun of suffering whales   planetary journeys
I begged for a machine-gun and was given a flower   poisoned
a yellow sun a blue and purple sun lying in a pool of blood

I counted one sun after another and my legs got covered with ants

I counted the ants and suns blinded me  Palestine with no Palestine

a blue acetylene sun died of frost  in the presence of a palm tree
in death one plus one makes three   a cactus ate me
there is an Arabian sun on Mount Arafat   a heap of cut legs
the sun is velvet-winged atomic bomb   nuclear face
who is preventing us from rising? the pimpled face of the moon.
a red sun a purple sun a green sun a thick sun
this tender fish within the sun and this corpse in the yellow lake
I gave my blessing to the dumps where extinguished suns were buried.

IX

The sun paces the sky like a trapped animal
Fat human faced pig never dimmed yellow sun   Hou hou hou
I saw chickens in the sun's eye I saw a dog   TORTURE !
BURN is the film thunder and sun over CUBA   a cargo of light Houuuuu

Beirut the Yellow in its forest of guns 12 and May and 75 MUTE SEWN CITY

The sun has its mouth stitched with barbed wire STOP butcher's Arab sun

A sun of iron walks in a forest of guns   an eye bursts open STOP
Ishi cried this morning   STOP I counted up to 5 STOP the sea is on the phone

yellow sun exterminated ancestor sun green spring purple sun quasar
the sun has fallen in anti-matter there where mornings go   ARCHANGEL
the sun spread in the acid city of Beirut burned with sulphur
More irreversible than death is the sun   Round cloth and rooster's head

They carried the sun on the back of a donkey to the top of the hill 1000 men came

A sun laid disfigured STOP   Two airplanes. STOP interminable ambulance

the pink column smashed the face STOP the stone column broke the spine

a purple sun seized with vertigo   speed in its protuberances

There is ultimate speed in the sun's hair 　　　Transfigured horse
And a dead person laid in her funeral bed head looking like a rotten orange

MAY is her name a yellow sun in her mouth latent counter-fire　　STOP
Each vertebra is an extinct sun　　　each eye a volcano　　　　each ear a crater
eye extinct volcano eye coffin closed on itself ear meteor
sunlike urine paper STOP purple sun STOP BLACK ANTS
an ambulance drives between two hedges of silence　　　black sun
a bullet over the ocean ponders over a useless gun　　　　my cigarette burns
a sun tattooed with our sins STOP sun ripped up by lightning STOP glaring neutrons

In the sky a solitary coffin is floating from one horizon to the other
a horse with lanterns for eyes carries the body in his mouth 　　rainbows are perfect

a militant sky aims its Kalachnikov at the earth　　●　　BANG !

X

A pink dove shattered a human face   A solar hair in its beak
a yellow sun stop a green sun stop a blue sun stop
I asked the sun not to dismantle my body unified for ever
the sun is bawling its heat. Bawling its pain   The sound of plants STOP
a yellow sun a vociferous sun a blue sun a sun oozing its electrodes

a crazy sun a yellow sun a palm tree blinking in the sun's eye
a sun-ambulance carries Christ to the insane asylum   Close to the monkeys

a yellow sun hates the color green a green sun hating plants Hou ! ! !
the sun swings from one universe to another STOP the sun swings from one universe to another

My right eye is a sun my left eye is a sun my ears two suns

my nostrils two suns   I have the sun on my forehead   STOP

my feet are two suns STOP EACH FINGER is a sun
a sun at each toe STOP a sun in the arms in the anus in the neck
my feet two suns my ears two suns my nostrils two suns
and this sun at the mouth cancer until the end of the stars

my belly is a sun ⊙   a sun is a system which starts at the heart
a sun is this milky way which runs out of my mouth whirling sun
         the sun bawls its heat the sun bawls its light the sun is LUCIFER
I WANT HIM TO BE DEAF AND DEAD HORIZONTAL AS A FELLED FOREST

a pink dove breaks the cloud through and through   the sun was waiting
a sun O ship   a sun O silence   a sun O copper

CHE GUEVARA HAS BECOME A BUSH WITH WHITE SAP
THE PACIFIC HAS BECOME A LAKE OF BLOOD STOP
I AM THE SOLAR-BELLIED INDIAN WHO PLUNGES BEIRUT IN A BATH OF LIGHT
DEAD IS THE BODY THAT THE SHADOWS CARRY UNDERGROUND

XI

A yellow sun a mad sun a quiet sun a red sun a a
Helios sun moon reduced to a sun between two rocks BOUM BOUM BOUME !
A solar wind pulls your teeth Hou ! Hou ! the future is a wind
a young boat on the wrinkles of the sea in the sun's eye VOYEUR !
the solar wind blows at 500 miles per second ! HOULA ! ! !
interplanetary circular dust accompanies the traveling whirling sun
the sun revolves in twenty-seven days and its pain affects me
I hurt at the sun's belly   the sun hurts at my belly O my love!
I love a yellow sun you love a blue sun he loves a red sun
the sun plays STOP the sun cries STOP the sun falls asleep STOP
A   maddeningly yellow   a wart on my nose   satellites
the sun waits for SOYOUZ the sun waits for APOLLO the sun is GARGARIN
Malevich's red sun followed his funeral convoy all the way to BEIRUT
Beirut ⟶ Hell   Beirut ⟶ sun   Beirut ⟶ Damascus   Beirut ⟶ Venus

shiftings of time shiftings of space on the navigation board of matter

Paris ⟶ Jupiter   New-York ⟶ Saturn   Bagdad ⟶ Mercury   STOP
the sun hates wishful travelers It explodes in anger. HOU ! HOU !

the sun carries its victory from star to star on the road to the Milky Way . . .

It goes out to dinner with a meteor   it drinks earthly alcohols
the sun burns out its sanity from cell to cell to reach an apotheosis
cosmic radiations travel in a black universe
I remain at the heart of the revolution in the silent City
Tammouz is July nailed on a sundial in a frozen bath.

XII

Sun tribal Head ◉　　sky-blue sun ◎　　The Hopi's swastika
I would love to place you in the heart of the night make the stone of your belly surge

the sun oscillates within a seven-mile radius O acoustical waves travelling!

Sound runs on the solar face!!! 140 miles a second! permanent and nuclear series

sun tribal Head bristling with cannons passenger of bloody ships
rapacious sun elephant leading the tribe to its death STOP slaughterhouse
the sun leads the children to the slaughterhouse ⌒⌒ Tell Zaatar to victory
the sun is happy ⊕　　young grass proliferates
a rapacious elephant leads the tribe to its slaughterhouse STOP
the cannon spits a sun every hour on the hour. the solar elephant tills the sky
the sun is vainly suspicious of armies ◉　　resounding bell
metal disk cutting the sky's membrane for a rain of blood
war in Beirut war in Marrakech war in Dubai war in Mossoul

white sun black sun white sun black sun white sun black sun . . .

I planted the sun in the middle of the sky like a flag
a yellow sun floats like a tattoo over an incandescent tree
the sun is a blind tribal chief STOP the sun is blind
When you are thirsty and hungry the sun   eats its children and sings
the sun quivers the sun wavers the sun rises the sun breathes
O the solar chant rising from the belly of millions of women!
the sun is a celestial fish possessed by a shapeless dizziness
the sun started on the road which leads the tribe to the slaughterhouse

XIII

7 thousand Arabs under siege thirsty blinded STOP extinct suns
There are tumors on the moon's craters and Mars' dunes
7 thousand Arabs in the belly of vultures STOP a yellow sun   in their eyes

O millenary hunger ⟶ O Canaan on the sun's map
Intense winds escaped from the nuclear furnace HOU ! HOU !

the sun burst STOP the sun swelled burst traveled !!!!! HOU !
the yellow sun is a bagful of pus collected with a spoon in the Arabs' wounds

the sun bag of pus the sun hospital cosmic and cadaverous flower

the sun coat of arms of the Arabs   armor of the Muslims   light of the comets
the sun is a sick child the sun is dying on the mountain
O solar funerals ⟵ hearse carried by Fedayeens dressed in black

O soldiers solar and nocturnal living on the banks of a sewer
O Camp of thyme and verbena carrion-smelling   Tell Zaatar

In the ravine that the Camp overlooks like a kingdom   O sun !
women children men play a solar and deadly game
Life's enemies came by day and by night
And the sun cried   Women children men everything is dead
Sulfuric Venus flared in the sky   HOU HOU HOU   the heat is stone-like
Oh how flat is the sea   She is laminated   Bread is a piece of steel

a yellow sun a black sun a red sun a white sun
the sun moves in our eyes   the sun is an Arab corpse
Sun of BABYLON   sun of GILGAMESH   sun of MOHAMMAD
A crater flowered in the desert's body STOP it is the SUN'S eye
Resurrection of the dead STOP Resurrection of the Planets STOP Resurrection of the peoples.

XIV

I advance as a white bird over your heads   With a sun in the belly

feet in the sand HOU ! HOU ! HOU ! Wind in my feet
I chose to wander STOP A yellow sun has risen on the Camp
a purple sun in Canaan's eye a green sun for Islam
a white sun on the fields of the future   a traveling shark
Oh! the sun is a shark pursuing stars in the sky's seas
I chose a tribal chief son of Andromeda and the Sun
the young king of Syria moves in the stormy instability of the skies
yellow sun blue sun tattoo in craters and wounds
They burned the chloroforms ate the antiseptics STOP They laughed
mercenary sun Arabian anti-sun BIG BLACK HOLE IN THE UNIVERSE
I climbed   the column   I climbed   the mountain
I climbed   the cloud   I climbed   the sun
And I saw: masked men execute a carnage
We have to drink blood in order to join them and wait for them in hell
O peaceful sun eternal father of Canaan's children
O Babylonian Deluge ancestor of the Arabs Wind Wind
One two three . . . messages stream from the computers
I sleep with a radio in my arms STOP I sleep at Tell Zaatar
At the door of Paradise STOP a solar bath
I see rockets among trees. Concrete catching fire
cages crumble smashing crushing merchants The cardinal points explode
Sleeps the horse innoculated with innocence under the madness of the Moon

XV

In the halls of the sun we manufactured virulent religions
We burned still-born children HOU ! HOU ! the solar goddess!
The brain is a sun STOP the sun is an eye

Each nuclear explosion blooms into a sun-brain like a flower !

Within the sun's atoms we created virulent races STOP
the sun's atoms are Moslem saints saints muezzins
We used a bistoury on each solar atom O sorrow !
the sun is an Indian snake a Sioux covered with light
Indians lead rounds in the heart of the sun STOP Vertigo!
Indians dance in their mothers' belly STOP yes ! yes!
Blinded angels are coming by the thousands carrying petroleum-spoked banners

Arabs are dancing in the dust DOUM !   the Tribe is delirious
the yellow sun   children's toy in the shanty-towns   is eating the sea
Each bullet is a ball planted in the brain YES !

XVI

Light comes on horse-back crosses the desert bathes the city
there is a paradise inside the yellow sun towards which the refugee is walking

There is a refuge only in death there is no refuge but in fire

the sun's atoms are incarnating in my flesh   STOP   STOP
DOUM ! DOUM ! DOUM !   the streets are covered with corpses whose mouths open to the spring

mouths full of teeth full of dust are shouting Allahu Akbar

the sun is the Tribe's ultimate god the sea is a shroud
They came with whetted swords to fight the sea

They drowned   the sun solar boat led them to the horizon.

XVII

Jupiter moves forward followed by thirteen moons   STOP   Ganymedes enamored of the sun

Beirut is a poultry yard with peacocks and the stench of poultries
Jupiter swims in a metallic solution   The discharge is incoherent

Beirut is a satellized planet domesticated by its enemy profanated by EVIL
An electric current covered with hair like a mare circulates in the universe
Beirut hides in trenches   bending its neck goes to the slaughter house

The BIG RED SPOT of Jupiter is a storm. Matter is desperate.
Beirut is eaten by civil war children listen to the roar of cannons
matter in fury turns in circles in the big void of the planets
Beirut wallows in misfortune HOU ! HOU ! HOU ! Beirut bleeds
matter circles in tornadoes on nebulae's surfaces   O Milky Way!
more blood than milk   more pus than wine
Jupiter defies the sun a yellow sun makes love to Jupiter
hatred is filled with phosphorus jealousy wears a black ribbon
Jupiter revolves within the boundaries of its acid madness
Beirut turns round and round it is a weathercock of disaster
Jupiter gets away from the sun and runs back to it: it is a hunting dog
any Arab crowd is a crowd of poets. Listen to its maledictions!
incandescent planets darkly flutter in the heart of the war

geomagnetic forces dry up our regions We implore the rain
we receive solar particles We want to see We are blind

We go in hordes to praise the Lord the solar Face is pitiless
Jupiter and the sun fight over Gilgamesh's mortal remains

XVIII

I see white solar emissions   radiations of thought blazing with fire

The sun has lived half its life   STOP   it stands at the center of the Scales

5 billion years on each side   5 billion Arabs hungered
Big blue tattoo on the galaxy's face   YES !   YES !   we are hungry
When Guatemala breaks down Indians become watermelon seeds

the sun glides the sun flies the sun swims the sun slides the sun runs away

an intermediary yellow sun   the yellow sun of menopause

This pupil in the big eye is the sun   stares at us intensely
We are Xrayed by the sun and the lies we tell are tumors
When Guatemala breaks under the teeth of the Earth they start laughing in Washington

LAUGHTER the sun is laughing LAUGHTER the sun is laughing LAUGHTER the sun is laughing

5 billion solar years   are grass snakes hiding in the texture of TIME

XIX

the universe is everywhere and its child-like patience protects us STOP
the universe's patience is a balm STOP a child's patience is a flower
a yellow sun took the place of the Arab's eye mouth and teeth
on the big ships of the Arabian Gulf they will sail like atoms
I think of the absolute freedom of the atoms in the sun's combustion

I wear the solar crown ☼ as a crown of sorrow. I'm walking !

O people with no calendar O Arab people O people unstable O phosphorescent people !

the sun is a fishermen's lake with burnt feet they swim!
a yellow sun stricken with menopause   O patience!
Sun! the day has come for you to be inoffensive   shapeless spinning top

THE SOLAR BOAT IN THE MIDDLE OF ITS COURSE GETS SIDETRACKED IN ORCHARDS
IN A PORCELAIN SKY STOP FULLSTOP STOP STOP

XX

Mercenaries brandish the sun   the sun itself is a mercenary
A YELLOW SUB bought in the market   STOP   ANGOLA SOLD TO JUPITER
the sun blood bath poured on the BUSH   STOP   the sun white mercenary

the sun's tentacles set Africa on fire   STOP   Arabs and Blacks are stabbed HOU !

an Apocalyptic sun explodes   I hear the cracking of bones
a mercenary sun in love with the Jungle warms the snakes
blue bath blood is pouring over the BUSH like a nocturnal Opera

SUNFLOWERS ARE SPINNING IN A SOLAR YARD STOP

the sun is an opera STOP morbid singers are climbing down the stairs
a sun yellow and soft. the sun is bald like a hot afternoon

POT-BELLIED MERCENARY AGING FEMALE THAT'S THE SUN

defeated androgyne androgynous sun clear androgyne
they're biting their swords to rip children and immigrants

I MADE LOVE TO A GUN UNDER THE SHADOW OF THE LAST PALM

sun spinning top incredibly spinning instead of our eyes
I dribbled your dissident particles made war to your wound
HOUM   HOUM   HOUM   mercenary covered with solar hair
I planted an Arab in the center of the sun like a fig tree
then I spat blood   got purified in urine

THE MERCENARY SUN SPENT THE SEASON WITH ME

XXI

the sun is ferocious its black center turns ceaselessly   STOP
the sun is ill its hair is falling in black space
the sun disoriented cosmonaut cuts the contact with Earth
the sun is losing its teeth   It lost its gum
the sun is a traitor traitor is the sun   FOR EVER
the sun spits the blood it sucked from scorpions
the sun drills holes in the brain of the Palestinian
the sun unites the Arabs against the Arabs
the sun married its mother to better crucify its son
the sun got dressed became a transvestite undressed disguised
the sun walks naked on a burning rolling mill
the sun heads the convoy leads light to catastrophe
the sun air pilot lands on the Enemy's runway as a friend
the sun sells its lineage as slaves at dawn and in the west . . .   ● ● ●

XXII

I am the prophet of a useless nation   STOP   the base of my brain hurts
Smohalla Tecumtha Smohalla Tecumtha Smohalla Tecumtha Smohalla
I am a sniper with glued hair on my temples   STOP
the sun is a frozen lemon as big as Presidents' noses
Each wounded is a dead man   Beirut is a corpse presented on a silver platter

the sorcerer ~~━━━━~~ sun blows into straws
Drinks lemonades in the cemetery's alleys
the sun has its phallus decorated with ribbons   STOP
I am the terrorist hidden in the hold of a cargo from Argentina
the sun is a shark faithfully following Uruguayan sailors
I am the judge sitting in every computer shouting FREEDOM IS FOR WHEN ?

the sun distributes the hours into bureaucratic drawers
The convicts drag themselves to the fountain of blood

Amidst a smell of corpses forgotten by the garbage collector sleeps the sun

while perspire the plants.

XXIII

The radio says History allocated 10 billion years to the sun
   the SUN has already lived half its age
morning sun evening sun you are pure you are pure
the sun insinuated itself into glycerine bags   the sun exploded

the sun emptied the drugstores   the sun is out for a walk in the desert

the sun takes drugs to commit its crimes   on the hills it takes drugs

the sun has ripped skins bellies feet and brains
And the trees!   Even the grains of sand exploded
Beirut capsized into the sun's heart   its spell annihilated it

We came with a sun instead of a face   sun hung on a tree

And decapitated columns cried   Babylon's women got slaughtered

History has pushed the accelerator of its power to infinity
villages fell as grains of dust   roses are dynamos
the sun has emptied all courtyards   drank the fountain's water
Gilgamesh has razed the Walls   the fields refuse to shelter the harvest
the sun has sat on the banks of the Orontes and of the Tigris   for ever
Gilgamesh has returned in an airplane to water us with petroleum
We washed our eyes in the solar inferno
Blind are the Arab kings who howl in the night
the sun is an eternal wind which became insane the morning of its first love

XXIV

BAUDELAIRE mercenary sun alphabet originated in Ugarit   King of Babylon
sun prince of words   STOP   THE VERB'S CREATION STOP
a yellow sun a word a sun choking my throat
between the Tigris and the Euphrates the sun is quivering
between the River Meuse and Spain a yellow sun remembers . . .
speech is made of solar particles   STOP   HOU ! HOU ! HOU !
Baudelaire mercenary selling his words to solar tribes as that many bullets!

sun knower of men the sun is a verb carried by our fingers
sun: herds of poets manifesting the dethroned power of words

BIG PHOSPHORESCENT RINGS CHAIN LANGUAGE TO THE TREE OF EVIL

a yellow sun   a blue sun   a black sun   the language-circuit has burned   STOP

Baudelaire mercenary Gerard de Nerval's assassin   STOP
sun Avicenna the hangman of Al Hallaj who was thrown to the gutters of Andalusia
the sun divested itself from its words in Dhofar for an intergalactic journey

XXV

It's raining on the sea STOP the fish open their Umbrellas to protect her

It's Anat it's Ishtar it's Isis it's Aphrodite on the look out for the male sun

the sun has risen on a damp arm STOP I gave birth to a dead city
the fish have eaten the corpses which float down the Mountain
on Mount Sannine the sun wept STOP Tears made of lead and petroleum
A sun red-and-blue brazier sacrificed a lamb in the city's arteries

The militiamen settled in the veins of my eyes
Boum Boum was the song and the infernal message
How many ghosts hide in the silence?
the fish disembark STOP settle down and give parties
A shark stays by the window The Whale sits on the THRONE
Sun fish swimming only in dried-up wells
Sun whale wrapped with electric wire HOU ! HOU ! HOU !
waters are running and earth is melting in a deluge: bowl of water
We return to the child who drowned in these solar rivers one morning
O Andalusia and Mari besieged by cosmic rays !
And lunar Beirut on its knees with its people in the belly
Fish back in their tank like so many fetuses ⸫ Winds
The silent march of Matter-Spirit in the body of the amputated
Is an eternal voyage.

XXVI

Who is it? It's Christ whose head turned into a white sun
His burial? Four planks and nails gathered in meadows
His mother? Dressed in lunar rays and white silence
His will? A 10 dollars bill posted in New York
His son? The product of the ox and the snake
His weapons? his fingernails hanging on the sun
His mother? the planet Saturn
His burial? the one of the neighbor who was made king by error
His son? the water-carrier the noise and the lightning
His will? a succession of tombs in the Center of Town
Who is it? It's Christ whose head wears a white bandage for ever
His daughter? WAR WITH NO REVOLUTION

XXVII

the sun always moves against the wind the sun revolves in cyclones
the sun lies on a table white walls undulate in the heat
the sun had its legs amputated O defeated mercenary!
flies are buzzing worms stink blood is turning white
They carried   the sun on their stretched arms to the cemetery
Escorted by its planets STOP the sun falls in the vortex of death

They cut the sun's ears and stuffed them in a jar
the smell of phenol contaminated the bread for the poor
the children played ball with the sun's dead body STOP
they put nails chains and metal bars in the sun's body
They came wearing masks STOP They came poisoned STOP They came castrated STOP

They gave a child a coffin to play with STOP
the yellow sun shrank amputated he called his mother
ISHTAR never answered STOP the Virgin never called STOP
IN the dead sun's body they hid their plunder
ON the city's highest tower they proclaimed the kingdom of DEATH
The archaic coast distributed to the waves the scattered organs of the solar disc STOP

XXVIII

Sun ⊙ ～～ DELAWARE ⟶ BEIRUT HELL
    THE SUN BROKE its cables   It's sliding towards a new abyss
One ●   two   three   four   five   six   seven   eight   nine
    1   2   3   4   5   6   7   8   9
the sun is the fighter's heavy load o o o o o o o o o o o o
    a boat crumbled under the sun's ⟶ weight
Incredible sun you took the road to EVIL
    a mad sun lost its hair standing on the hill
    BEIRUT HEADING TOWARD THE FISHERMEN'S WHITE INFERNO
O incredulous harvest the sun broke loose to take us in its arms !

To the red hot table the Palestinian is soldered
    the sun broke its cables   1   2   3   4
Trees with fiery fingers are monstrously swelling
a senile sun dribbles over the plants and straddles his sister
The moon barks to rouse the clouds ～～～⟶STOP
Follows a rain of bullets
O desert infinite and vaster than the sun and jealous of my memory!
1 dried well 2 dried wells 3 dried wells 4 dried wells . . . .
    ● the sun broke its silence for a chain of maledictions

XXIX

the sun is   unsettled   dissident   eruptive   in anarchy
I forbade the sky to traverse my eyes STOP Running
They came with yellow ears and drained nostrils
I saw cross-bearers with   death in their sockets
the boys cried   TOP the girls didn't spread the linen
the father died of a heart-attack on a boat named Cyprus
the mother was beating raw meat the enemy surged from the stone mill
She ate with cannibal eagerness the icons and the bread
Then sang a sour litany on Resurrection Sunday
the sun-muezzin intonated prayers till the evening of palms
the mother and the recitant met in the fire
I saw them throw their cut-up fingers on the Church's platter
The saints did not come to their rescue the Companions neither
between two epic pauses they fought believe it!
the sun's pain rose on the thermometer
muezzins and priests posted bulletins of victory
the combatants remained horizontal on the horizontal line of the sea

XXX

Rider of clouds   sun Syrian worker   proto sinaïtic
What a purple and violent abyss broke loose on the Primordial land of Syria?

What an ancestral love out of the infinite and the universe had to reside in your belly?

I smothered the sun with an iron bar   disfigured its words   tore its face

And mine. Big black holes. Quasars ! the others' death in Beirut SHHHH

the sun is on its way to extinction. STOP splinters from shells or solar splinters?

Little pieces of death Pieces of Osiris' body dispersed while Great Isis is absent HOU !

Great Isis is absent STOP I am the root that her tomb crushed STOP
My planet-like face is pockmarked by miserable particles of lead

my grandfather is giving a last battle in an abyss inhabited by bats

In the land of Adonis raspberries bleed as much as we do.
a yellow sun   a yellow sun   a yellow sun   a yellow sun
the sea quivers under its mobile corpses   man is slaughtered more than sheep

Baal-Sun Thunder and black rain   the sea gave birth to snakes
lightning breaks through the city's towers   electricity oozes from our eyes

How can we exorcise malediction when we ourselves are cursed?
What to do with the sun when it hides behind tear gas?
Drink it. Drink it in little sips so that tenderness resembles hell.

XXXI

Beirut is closed to the human tide STOP the Harbor sank
There is no sap left in the trees for the people's thirst
A forest of cactus shelters iron birds STOP houses lose their arms

A sun yellow with anger rummages   in the corpses' bellies
the combatants curse the heat which filters through their eyelashes
flies buzz like helicopters above dry fountains

I ate dragon-flies from morning to night STOP HOU ! ! ! ! ! ! !
dog-shaped ghosts sleep in dumpsites
the earth spits noxious rays as if they were words
the sun is a deaf star STOP the sky is its tomb
the new cavemen dribble lead
the sea is a blue and white shroud STOP the drapers left town

the witch-doctors gave their scalping tools to the liberated prisoners
the latter are cutting the head of whoever goes by
the human tide barks at the door of the palm groves STOP
There is no bread no water no air no light
There is death's warm coat and nothingness
And when their weapons fall with fatigue they fight with their nails.

XXXII

Pontiac Faysal Pontiac Faysal Pontiac Faysal Pontiac Faysal Pontiac
the sun drank the victory pissed it out in the Mississippi
warm seas are full of rotten algae and woolly birds
red is the sun at sunset as at sunrise and bitter
a yellow lemon between its teeth and its phallus exposed
the young king of Arabia is bathing in oil
his mouth is shiny and black his teeth sink in petroleum
his eyes are becoming blind inch by inch like distorted suns
the sea is a belly dilated to receive the still-born
Indians and Arabs give battle backwards backwards
Gold powder covers the fighters betrayed by their own
There is in every tribe a gold-thirsty traitor
There is in every Arab a traitor thirsting for the West
Pontiac and Faysal hand in hand sleep in the sunset
the last king of the humiliated races remains lain on the horizon

XXXIII

The Arabs' sun   is a perennial atom bomb drinking milk sadistic tubercular

with its fingers sewn the sun caresses the Euphrates
It runs and multiplies from the Atlantic to the Gulf to smash a blade of grass

a tattooed sun eats the hand that helps it to rise
It hurries from Baghdad to Beirut to rip up 8000 horses
on the pine forests a sickly sun drops pesticides
it hunts the gazelle from a motorcycle
a rachitic sun marries the Bedu woman to beget a deformed child
It goes to sea to only decimate blue sharks
a sun ball of smoke puts harbor after harbor on fire STOP black smoke
It eats up wheat silos in front of hungry mouths
a cholera-stricken sun moves in the Camp's labyrinth
it tortured the Palestinian fighters already gunned down on a bed of dirt

a sun filled with glory drinks the shanty towns' sewers STOP FULLSTOP
it pretends to be king and whips improbable slaves
. . . . a faltering sun implores the Mountain
a venimous sun buys jewelry in the Great Capitals
It escorts a herd of beggars to the Friday prayers. dismembers Syria
a sun gone insane chases its tail on the Market Place
The sun dips into an eclipse and crepuscular gloom

XXXIV

Oh no! the amorous storm sets in the West
the sun sings by candlelight the sad victory laid out on the slabs

a man has died in Beirut a woman too
it's their first night of rest in a long time
Tecumtha Indian warrior climbs on Mount Arafat
6000 men 100 tanks decimate the Companions of the Resistance
Oh how cold is the ground in full summer when it is watered with blood!
Jisr el Basha got ready for the Revelation Tell Zaatar perfumed with flowers
a young man and his beloved die hand in hand
the bride is welcomed by the sun the moon covers the adolescent with praise
they sleep together on their bed riddled with bullets for ever! for ever!

XXXV

ONE yellow plane transformed into a sun goes faster than the sun
ONE yellow mercenary crawls under the stones all the way to the Hill
ONE wounded man a hole in his forehead walks under the sun
yellow worms crawl out of the hole the air is warm

STOP STOP STOP STOP STOP STOP STOP STOP STOP STOP STOP

a sun airborn a sun ⎯⎯⎯airplane circles up there . . . ⎯⎯⎯⟶
there is no water ●   no plasma ●   no air there is the radio
there are star fish streaking in the night
the Tuaregs arrive motorized empty-handed

HOU ! HOU ! HOU ! HOU ! HOU . HOU . HOU ! HOU ! HOU ! HOU ! HOU !

Libya disappears under tornadoes of sand
Egypt buries the solar Pharaoh under spit
only the Yakima Indian washes our forehead
the besieged Palestinians walk on all four
the Great solar Circle has encircled them in its iron ring
And tired of words they begin to bark

XXXVI

In the dark irritation of the eyes there is a snake hiding

In the exhalations of Americans there is a crumbling empire

In the foul waters of the rivers there are Palestinians

OUT OUT of its borders pain has a leash on its neck

In the wheat stalks there are insects vaccinated against bread

In the Arabian boats there are sharks shaken with laughter

In the camel's belly there are blind highways

OUT OUT of TIME there is spring's shattered hope

In the deluge on our plains there are no rains but stones

XXXVII

Windblown seconds are swelling the tide It's the sadness of wind-bags
Drinking wine I drink blood and lie next to an inanimate body

I go down the stairs of the Divine Comedy under Tell Zaatar's tell

seconds are filled with sands and tears and eyes are planted with fern

Doomed is the DAY DOOMED DUM DUM SPLASH AND DOOM
They killed the dream with an axe! with an axe! with an axe!
I go down a waterless river in front of mercenaries
Their hatred is a laser their glances are descents into hell
The killed fedayi's bride lost her arm and her leg
On the horizon children are advancing as birds on the move

The sun has spent the night underground ● among the insane and the sick
and I saw caterpillars as long as elephants

XXXVIII

A clear morning of cold rocks lost on an oceanic trail . . .
a lighthouse calls the tide of Palestinians branded with red
their guts protrude as umbilical cords

    savage is the enemy who settles in their eyes STOP O sorrow!
    the sun spinal cord ending in liquefied brains
    active death livelier than life but black and surgical
    the solar stone-column falling on the martyr's head
    Fedayeen of a still-born cause of a sun born from anti-matter
    in the big holes of SPACE mortuary chambers are being prepared
    the Palestinians are dumped in a space-craft heading for the moon
    They sing their own requiem in the launched rocket
    piloted by the angels of EVIL in outer Space they get lost
    stone has no memory STOP the sun neither STOP
    on the market-place a bull is slaughtered in their stead
    the Taurus' horns say Spinning Palestine
    between sunflowers and tops there is eternal quarrel
    an airplane is circling the Earth without ever landing
    the blood-stained Sun is presiding in the PRISONS

XXXIX

When the living rot on the bodies of the dead
When the combatants' teeth become knives
When words lose their meaning and become arsenic
When the aggressors' nails become claws
When old friends hurry to join the carnage
When the victors' eyes become live shells
When clergymen pick up the hammer and crucify
When officials open the door to the enemy
When the mountain peoples' feet weigh like elephants
When roses grow only in cemeteries
When they eat the Palestinian's liver before he's even dead
When the sun itself has no other purpose than being a shroud

the human tide moves on . . .

XL

the sun is a camera which operates only in black and white
white white white is the color of Terror
from their eyes nothing remains but egg-white and trees! blackness
in the underground blackroom always black is   experience

the sun is counting the earth's rotations   automobile wheel
and on the Palestinian's head rolls a truck
a concrete roof collapsed on 500 bodies
and the sun took the picture for the C.I.A.'s archives
sun camera majestic lens Prince of the gaze
white white white is the result of the sun's clicking
when teeth become as white as eyes
the sun executioner focal point of death goes into action
blood has no color in the torture-chambers
infrared rays make writings on the calcinated bodies of the Arabs

XLI

Arabs are the red algae which gives its muscle to the Ocean

a worker flies from hill to hill STOP follows the bees STOP

he's a pearl diver STOP he fishes out cartridges By God!
his bread is made of iron his water is his mother's pee
he'll wander from wall to wall
in solar spits he'll read his itineraries
they'll throw garbage in front of his former home
his brain will explode under a beam of light
he'll get transformed into a solitary mute will be anonymous and tattooed
      Arabs are red roots bleeding on a concrete floor

XLII

Sitting in the Sun's center I am guided by continents
Arabs live lives which go by in elephant lines
O millenniums of marches and water searches!
O caravans of hunger and curiosity O passion for Space!
and the species' submission to the cardinal virtues of Time
the infectious throbbings of America's bliss have flowered the sky with parachutes

how to forget the rockets gone to Venus and Mars ? !
O solar crucifixion and powerlessness of the most brilliant of the stars!
between love and the tenuity of seconds the sun is trapped

XLIII

I climbed the highest tower to look into the sun
My hair caught fire My eyebrows burned! But I saw
tornadoes covered with flames storms viscera circles of magic
The sun put its head into its hands filled with tears   O yellow victory!

Its face is eaten by salt STOP it is self flagellating
in lava are sitting nakedly spinning dervishes banned from a summer garden

under the obscene thighs of angels miserable beings are waiting
should we love the poor the left out the rebels and the oppressed?
I married a river to eat its fish cannibal ! cannibal !
no one met any tenderness nothing which is alive knows how to love
bald malicious women are feeding the fire
they came out of the furnace with white ears and burst eyes

I climbed on the Tower of Spits O yellow sun ! O blue sun !
we all sat down around a burnt out meal
hatred fought hatred recognizing Absolute Evil to be Absolute
the sea spat its pus on our beaches and in our mouths
the sun's throat is a tunnel which swallows our ARMIES
desire is dispersed on wheat fields. I saw castles planted between two graveyards

XLIV

Where do you want ghosts to reside?
In our wakeful hours there are flowers which produce nightmares
We burned continents of silence   the future of nations
the breathing of the fighters got thicker   became like oxen's

there is in that breath sparkles of scorched flesh and the fainting of stars

we crucify Gilgamesh on a TANK Viking II reaches Mars
Imam Ali dances over a nuclear blast
cursed are the clouds which repel water
cursed are the Arabs who fell tall and haggard eucalyptus trees

XLV

We all are future corpses   the sun like you is covered with flowers

Eye of Baudelaire haunted by violence   Divine eye haunted by matter
we are future astronauts gone to lunar funerals
the last assault is broken on the Tell the smell of thyme portends evil !
continents broke away from their moorings 1.2.3.4.5. A horse swallows its teeth

a yellow sun a green sun an extinguished sun a green sun a yellow sun a

The poet came with blind words and empty pockets C D E F

Eye of Baudelaire mercenary back from Angola shipped by cable
Eye of Ibn el Fared back from the Thames and spiked in Jounieh-by-the-Sea
the grave diggers used coffins to build houses

on every branch the militia hung severed heads
they dug out the dead   cut their organs and stuffed their mouths

One's cruelty was helped by the others' cruelty Destiny has been derailed

on the wires travelling doves read messages
the radio gave the numbers and television the colors
I breathed the breath of the plague and they chased me out of the camp
throwing stones at me throwing stones throwing stones
the living had slept 59 days with the corpses 59 days 59 days
not counting the nights and the hours

XLVI

There are more Syrian kings in the ant-hills than ants   STOP THEM !
They drank drops of sweat and infants' blood
the invaders arrived with cameras followed by a huge solar laughter

I pushed a body into a well and it talked back to me with a Palestinian accent

I was scared a fighter arrived running and planted a flag and a sword

the Syrian kings stood one by one   left their well for another well

the sun came down from the sky to inspect the Underground STOP it went back nauseated

the Syrian kings went into the second well on all four on all four

I was scared a fighter arrived perched on a tank STOP saluting
each leader's eldest son played ball with his younger brother STOP

the American ambassador arrived with a bullet in the back! and crutches

the sun got subdued with tranquilizers   started chewing grass
young men began hopping in their labyrinths shouting: everything stinks!
yes said the sun your consciences stink too as well as your tattooings
the Syrian kings tried to get out of their well no said the sun I'm blue

the sun cut their toes and told the Palestinians: this is your dinner

XLVII

I want people to call God "our brother" our "brother"
O celestial comrade born of the Night and of Light ! STOP
O celestial comrade receive your brothers in your eternity
O celestial comrade write their name on their burnt limbs
O celestial comrade give water and bread to the hungry
O celestial comrade give fuel to the friendly airplane
O celestial comrade please the widows by evoking their husbands

O celestial comrade allow brides to ignore the sounds of war

O celestial comrade reunite the combatants' dispersed bones

O celestial comrade erase the blackness of mourning and plant rose bushes
O celestial comrade sing a requiem of glory for those whose voice is sealed in tombs

XLVIII

They sleep under wild mulberry as if they themselves were roots
the non invisible sun broils their eyes STOP They came by night
Which night?   the one which outlasts the sky
let the lack of bread become a fabulous song!
the sheep share their wool and the woolf its anger
snakes come to help airplanes sting those who sleep

under the haggard gaze of black stars STOP in the smell of manure
from the banana fields the stench of despair rises in the air
there is no dialogue save between stones STOP   apples are put to sleep

pentothal is reserved for the Army   torture for the innocent
our eyes stare at the sea
refuse and crashed airplanes swim under the sun
I saw camels harnessed to the U.S.A. and going at 200 miles an hour
for one hour for one hour   dust has devoured all . . .
they climbed to the top of their tents to look at the future
Death wearing her ornaments arrived on her horse for a very long halt

XLIX

When the madness of the peoples of the world knocks at the door we go down and open . . . .

but to see them agitate their sea-colored kites
They claim bread but also and mainly the purity of waters
And the purity of eyes STOP they demand mornings to outnumber nights
But weary of counting the tombs of the sun's glory
they fold their blankets while the weather is cold HOU !
They go on foot under a sky inhabited by space rockets
their tongue is cooler than dew ~~their~~ their nostrils are humid

spring rambles at their sight STOP the harvest is accelerated
the houses follow the epic march
they are also moving for the very first time
rivers are playing invented instruments
And under the blue clouds of Babylon turtle-doves announce a thunder
1   2   3   1   2   3   1   2   3
the thunder of a war which needs not generals

L

There have been pounds and pounds of decomposed flesh   tons of suffering

Millions of dollars of pain   tons of crushed flesh
There have been mountains of corpses and rivers of blood
Bags filled with bones   baskets filled with eyes   bowls filled with lymph
There have been meadows covered with human skin under the Arabian moon

Millions of dollars of hatred and tons of sorrow
There have been yellow shells over the mourning of disemboweled houses
Tons of despair and gigantic rivers filled   with our collective tears

LI

When in a last slumber wake and garden are evoked
pain's emissaries reach our eyelids

when the sun does justice to life and death in the middle of the sky
a mask of steel descends over its face
the soldiers play a game of marbles with extinguished stars O Great Tattoo-maker!
The asphalt swells Runs into their mouths Grease is EVIL
Within the reflexions of black surfaces and in yellow mirrors I fall asleep
the wake and the garden enter through the window
armored vehicles smash the sun's fortress
submarines aim their turret guns at the planet Venus
but coded messages continue to arrive by the end of the hour
They give the name of the soldiers poisoned by raspberries
           night weighs on my eyes and blows hard into my nostrils light on light

LII

The sun has 52 vertebrae They hanged it by its neck It has 52 vertebrae
Trinity of doom Rope for the Apocalypse a wet and thoughtful sky
A yellow sun a blue sun a red sun legs which number six
the sun has numbers in its food and ropes which number three
Trinity of pain I see pink roofs and restless turtle-doves
the great clouds migrate to the north september blows into winter
They left together they went to heaven at the tip of a rope
Do you know the smell of soap that accompanied their death ? HOU
         the sun's spinal cord remains for ever suspended
Between sky and earth three Palestinians are sailing
like slow fish half earthbound half celestial they circle Mother Earth

HOU!! HOU!! HOU!! HOU!! HOU!! HOU!! HOU!!

They enter through our ears and exit through the mouth HURRAH !!!
the ropes had been thinned with soap to make torture hygienic
the executioner washed his hands not to contaminate the victims
On Damascus' Main Square three trees grew in four hours
the generals were on time the tourists at their windows
the people the people the people were saying Praised be Hell !

LIII

There has been battle between carrions and corpses   I've been in love with a corpse

They tied him by the hair to the old Chevrolet   gun fire ! gun fire !
Legs still apart his genitals offered offerings beets
his back scratched the asphalt children applauded
    the sun long ago deserted the women's faces
The latter said: the Palestinian never suffers enough nor does the Armenian
the neighborhood had a name: BADAOUI   the month was August   the day Saturday
I saw dark skinned men wear hunting boots and soft jackets
the donkeys and the pigs refused their company HOU ! HOU ! HOU !
A woman a different shoe on each foot looked at them
More beautiful than the Virgin more heavily built   more tender in her heart
Larger than seas oceans and continents
They laughed They laughed They laughed Ignoble They laughed They laughed They laughed

LIV

Absence Absence Absence Absence Absence   Death to those who keep waiting
Great lunar journey Great subterranean journey Great solar journey HOU ! ! !
Occult absence and presence Terror put into capsules   Mouth of the Sea
I took the women by the hand and settled them in the South
Packs of hounds came to lay at their feet
the trees went up the terraces to admire the rockets
I vanquished the drought and predicted the Deluge. The Tigris and the Euphrates disappeared

the women went much further the enemy started to cry
the sea vomited its octopus on the Greek coast   Syria trembled
it is by peeling onions that cities fall stone on stone
They locked them up in cages. They knocked down airplanes
They put them on helicopters: they crawled on their bellies
placidly we put the stars away under blankets
death to those who do not replace their eyes with electric bulbs
it's the sea that follows funerals . . . standing up!
in the narrow fields there are those who expect dawn to break
       a knowledge made of mercy covers the tombs
       herds are being slaughtered in lieu of rivers
petroleum is used in the evening and for the night's apotheosis
anonymous combatants hustle the live and the dead in their will to reach the future

History is dead. the sun is Nothingness. the air is burning for ever.

LV

MAO or the new Rimbaud MAO or the new Rimbaud MAO or the new Rimbaud
O vigor of the sun in the crossing of the Yang-Tse swimming
MAO is the new Rimbaud walking throughout a solar year
O vigor of the sun in its flight from the Ardennes to Aden
MAO is double-son of Arabia whom Rimbaud carries on his back
hand in hand Rimbaud and MAO end up in the Harrar
They sign power pacts and walk in the bush
MAO crosses Lebanon on foot and the Rub al Khali on a bicycle
But it is on foot that he crosses the Great Desert of Syria
Which takes him with Rimbaud with Rimbaud to the Great Wall of China

LVI

Sounds of laughter are back on target   Sunken suns
we find strength in carrying flowers to disemboweled corpses
the sea licks the ballast and the rails of the cosmic train
demented women stand alone under the moon's noise   ERRANCE in the basilica
bodies buried at the start of the century and momified with salt are digged out
with their legs thrown apart bodies cry the absence of their sexual parts
They will not reproduce in the other world   will not make love to laurel trees
I said that this tongue   smoking like roast-lamb   will disappear
make tomorrow's men speak in signs   collectively
They threw the Arabic language to the garbage   toads took it up
Rivers will be abundant but solitary   the mountains too
eclipses will descend on earth to eat grass   wisely
a plate and fried eggs for the prophet's assassin
from valley to valley under the subterranean sand we'll wait
Spring will refuse to come   Earth will not have seasons anymore

LVII

the sun has sulfuric dreams   is growing a dark horn
his mouth painted with lime an Arab drinks the horse's water
the sun gets lost in dunes the world is in darkness
the monkey in the coconut tree wears ties and pants   government officials too
hasn't the sea told you that its power doesn't work anymore?
a fish dies in the belly of another fish also dying on Arabia's map
amputated they had to cross the desert on the naked bones of their legs
and above all had to avoid crying like puppies newly born
the sun has burned the lips of the poets   these smile with their teeth
roses went mad   they bleed in public places
killers are condemned to praise the beauty of the sea
sons make their beloved mothers pregnant   twirling suns
during the whole length of the war we saw the sun go for mountain walks
it distributed books to the blind   guns to the one-armed men
in the cellars it drank the acid wine of the Bekaa STOP
it jammed the trails of the Milky Way
the Arabs−astronomers   follow the wrong stars and when night falls
they say: here is the beginning   the day   and the victory

LVIII

Oil wells will dry out and eight-headed monsters will crawl on Earth
neither the cross of David nor the star   will resist the yellow waves
yellow is the color of plague yellow is the sun's color
palm trees will fall in front of the electric organs
the banners of death float on the pylons
the desert will be covered with concrete   springs sequestered by angels carrying blue swords
mountains of ice will melt in a boiling sea of salt
people's tongues will turn into tongues of fire
on the Throne of Goodness there will be a mute-deaf
in the seat of Evil we shall install an old mummy
throats will choke with gold   iron safes used as coffins
And rats will inherit the Heralded Kingdom.

LIX

When the sun will run its ultimate road
fire will devour beasts plants and stones
fire will devour the fire and its perfect circle
when the perfect circle will catch fire no angel will manifest itself STOP
the sun will extinguish the gods the angels and men
and it will extinguish itself in the midst of its daughters
Matter-Spirit will become the NIGHT
in the night in the night we shall find knowledge love and peace

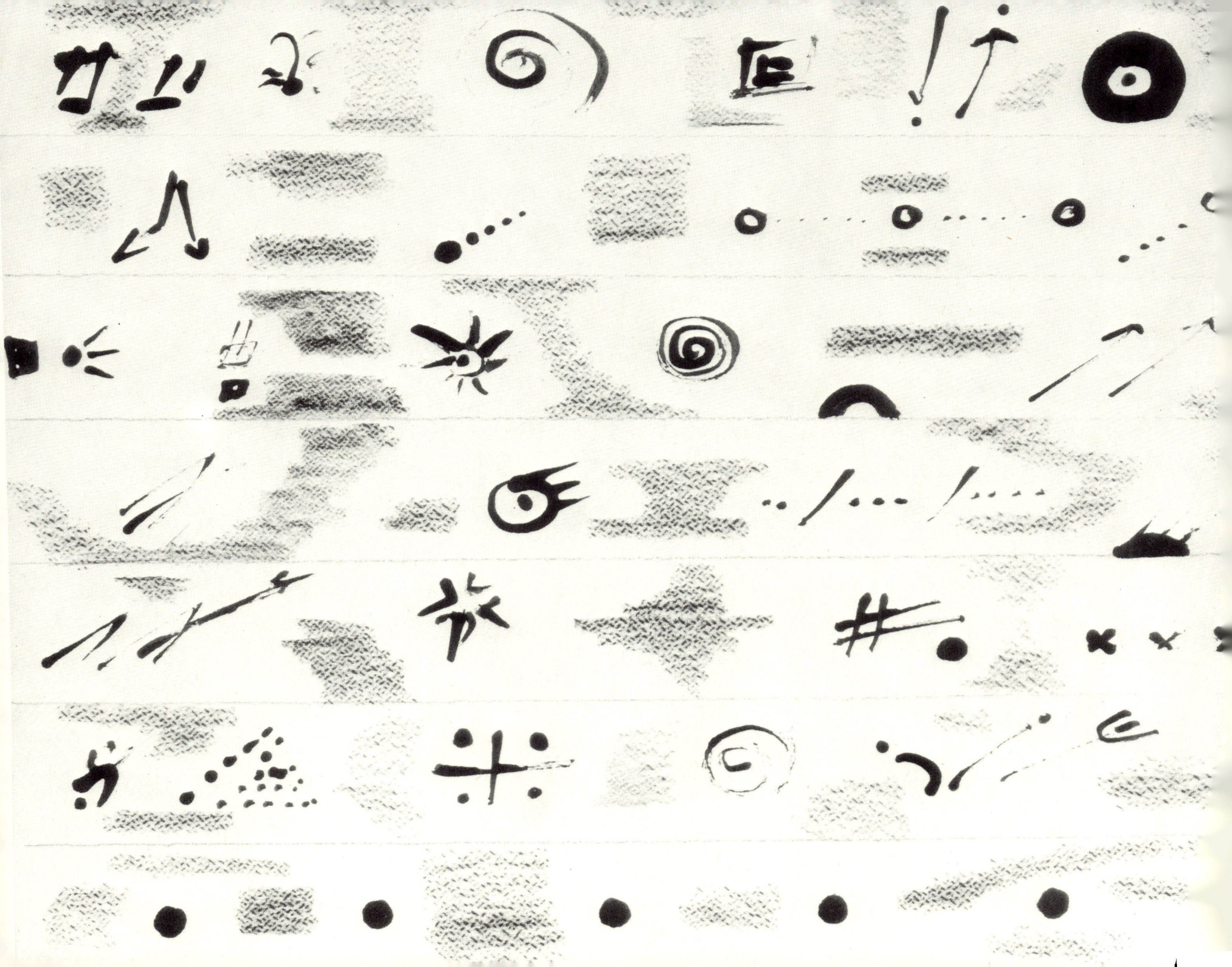